little bee books

A division of Bonnier Publishing
853 Broadway, New York, New York 10003
Copyright © 2016 by Bonnier Publishing
All rights reserved, including the right of reproduction in whole or in part in any form.
LITTLE BEE BOOKS is a trademark of Bonnier Publishing Group, and associated colophon is a trademark of Bonnier Publishing Group.
Manufactured in the United States   LB 0716
First Edition 10 9 8 7 6 5 4 3 2 1

Library of Congress Cataloging-in-Publication Data:
Names: Ohlin, Nancy, author. | Simó, Roger, illustrator.
Title: Blast Back! : World War II / by Nancy Ohlin ; illustrated by Roger Simó.
Other titles: World War II
Description: First edition. | New York, New York : little bee books, 2016. | Series: Blast Back! |
Includes bibliographical references. | Audience: Ages 7-10. | Audience: Grades 4-6.
Subjects: LCSH: World War, 1939-1945—Juvenile literature.
Classification: LCC D743.7 .O38 2016 | DDC 940.4—dc23
LC record available at https://lccn.loc.gov/2015049673

Identifiers: LCCN 2015049673
ISBN 9781499802757 (pbk) | ISBN 9781499802764 (hc)

littlebeebooks.com
bonnierpublishing.com

WORLD WAR II

by Nancy Ohlin   illustrated by Roger Simó
cover art by Adam Larkum

little bee books

CONTENTS

Introduction

Have you ever heard people mention World War II and wondered what they were talking about? Was the whole world really involved in the same war at the same time? What were the countries fighting about? Who sided with whom? And what was the outcome?

Let's blast back in time for a little adventure and find out. . . .

BLAST BACK!

10

World War II

A Brief History of World War II

You're wondering: What exactly *was* World War II?

World War II was a war that started in 1939 and ended in 1945. The words "world war" refer to the fact that nearly every part of the world was involved. "Two" refers to the fact that another world war took place before it. Many of the same countries fought in both world wars, but they were not always on the same side. Some of the events of World War I led to World War II. Both wars changed and shaped the course of history.

The countries that fought in World War II fell into two main coalitions, or groups: the Allied powers (also called the "Allies") and the Axis powers. The major Allied powers were Great Britain, the Soviet Union (which has since been divided into different countries), the United States, China, and France (except during the years when

France was occupied, or controlled, by Germany). There were dozens of other countries on the side of the Allies, including Canada, India, Nicaragua, New Zealand, and South Africa. The major Axis powers were Germany, Italy, and Japan.

World War II is also known as the Second World War and WWII.

BLAST BACK!

16

The World Before World War II

A lot was going on in the world in the years before World War II—including World War I, the birth of the Soviet Union, and the Great Depression.

World War I began in July of 1914 and ended in November of 1918. Most of the fighting took place in Europe, Russia, and in the Middle East. The winning side was called the Allies (although they weren't the exact same Allies that fought together in World War II). The main Allied countries in World War I were the United States, France, Great Britain, Russia, Japan, and Italy. The losing side was called the Central powers, which included Germany and the Austro-Hungarian Empire. (Today, Austria and Hungary are separate countries.)

In January of 1919, representatives of the Allies met in Versailles, France, to draft a peace treaty. Through the treaty, they created an organization called the League of Nations. One of the primary goals of the League of Nations was to prevent another world war.

The Treaty of Versailles was not favorable to Germany, which the Allies considered to be the main "bad guys" in the war. It forced the Germans to take the blame for the war, give up territory,

SOVIET
UNION

reduce the size of their military, and pay a lot of money to the Allies. The Germans protested but signed the treaty anyway.

In 1922, the Russian Empire became the Union of Soviet Socialist Republics, and it adopted communism as its form of government. With communism, the government controls the economy; the citizens are expected to give their money and other belongings to the government so it can be spread out evenly among everyone in the community.

The Union of Soviet Socialist Republics, also known as the Soviet Union, was the largest country in history until it ceased to exist in 1991; geographically, it was more than twice the size of the United States. It was also one of the most powerful countries in the world before (and after) World War II, and it had a major impact on the course of the war.

Another important world event around that time was the Great Depression. The Great Depression was a period of very tough economic times. It started in the United States in 1929 and spread around the world. Millions of people suffered from poverty, hunger, homelessness, and unemployment. ("Unemployment" means not having a job.)

The Rise of Nazism and Fascism

After World War I, Germany was not in good shape financially or otherwise. The German people blamed their government and sought a change in leadership.

A new political group called the German Workers' Party formed in 1919. Under Adolf Hitler, the group grew in power and became known as the Nazi Party. In 1920, Hitler created a program that outlined the Nazi agenda. Among other things, it stated that the Treaty of Versailles should be ended; that Germany should expand its territory; that one supreme leader with absolute power should rule the country; and most disturbingly, that certain groups, including Jews, were inferior and a threat to Germany and should be eliminated.

In the late 1920s and early 1930s, the Great Depression hit Germany and made things even worse for its citizens. Many turned to the Nazi Party to solve their problems. In 1933, Hitler became the chancellor, or prime minister, of Germany. He then established himself as the dictator, or absolute ruler, and he began to do away with anyone or anything that interfered with his goals.

At the same time, in Italy, another dictator had come into power: Benito Mussolini. His form of government was called fascism.

Like Nazism, fascism held that the state, or nation, was all-powerful and that individuals had no rights; those who disagreed or defied the laws were punished severely. And like the Nazi agenda, the fascist agenda included conquering other countries. Unlike Nazis however, fascists were not obsessed with racial and religious inferiority and superiority. Their most important priority was the authority of the government over its people.

Joseph Stalin

Hitler and Mussolini weren't the only dictators who played major roles in World War II. Joseph Stalin ruled the Soviet Union from the mid 1920s until his death in 1953.

Stalin was determined to turn the Soviet Union into a major world power as well as an industrial power with lots of factories and manufacturing. He took the ownership of individual farms away from the farmers and put the government in charge of them. Those who resisted his policies were killed or sent away to gulags. (Gulags were prisonlike camps where people were forced to perform hard labor under terrible conditions.) Stalin was responsible for millions of civilian deaths during his rule.

The Use of Propaganda

Propaganda is information, often inflated or misleading, that is used to convince people of a point of view. The Nazis used propaganda in World War II to persuade German citizens that the Allied powers, as well as the Jews, were evil and that the war was necessary.

Die Fahne des Sieges

When Hitler came into power, he established a Reich Ministry of Public Enlightenment and Propaganda, and appointed a man named Joseph Goebbels as its head. Goebbels spread the Nazi message through radio, newspapers, movies, plays, music, books, art, and other means. Those who disagreed with the propaganda were censored. (This means that their point of view was not allowed to be made public.)

The United States and Great Britain also used propaganda during World War II to rally support for their war efforts.

32

The War Begins

Several acts of military aggression around the globe led to the beginning of World War II.

Starting in 1931, Japan led a series of attacks against China. The Japanese wanted to expand their empire and gain more territory and power. These attacks erupted into a full war between the two countries in 1937.

In 1935, Mussolini's troops invaded the East African country of Ethiopia. In April of 1939, Italy also occupied the European country of Albania. A month later, Italy and Germany became allies by signing the Pact of Steel. (Japan joined later, in 1940, and the three countries came to be known as the Axis.)

In March of 1936, Hitler defied the Treaty of
Versailles and sent troops into the Rhineland,
which was the area between Germany and France.
Two years later, his troops seized Austria. In March
of 1939, they took over all of Czechoslovakia (which
is now two countries, the Czech Republic and the
Slovak Republic).

Poland was the next target on Hitler's list. France and Britain promised to come to Poland's aid if Germany invaded. Hitler didn't want to have to fight the French *and* the British *and* possibly the Soviet Union. So in August of 1939, he made an alliance with Stalin.

Weeks later, on September 1, 1939, Germany attacked Poland. That marked the official start of World War II.

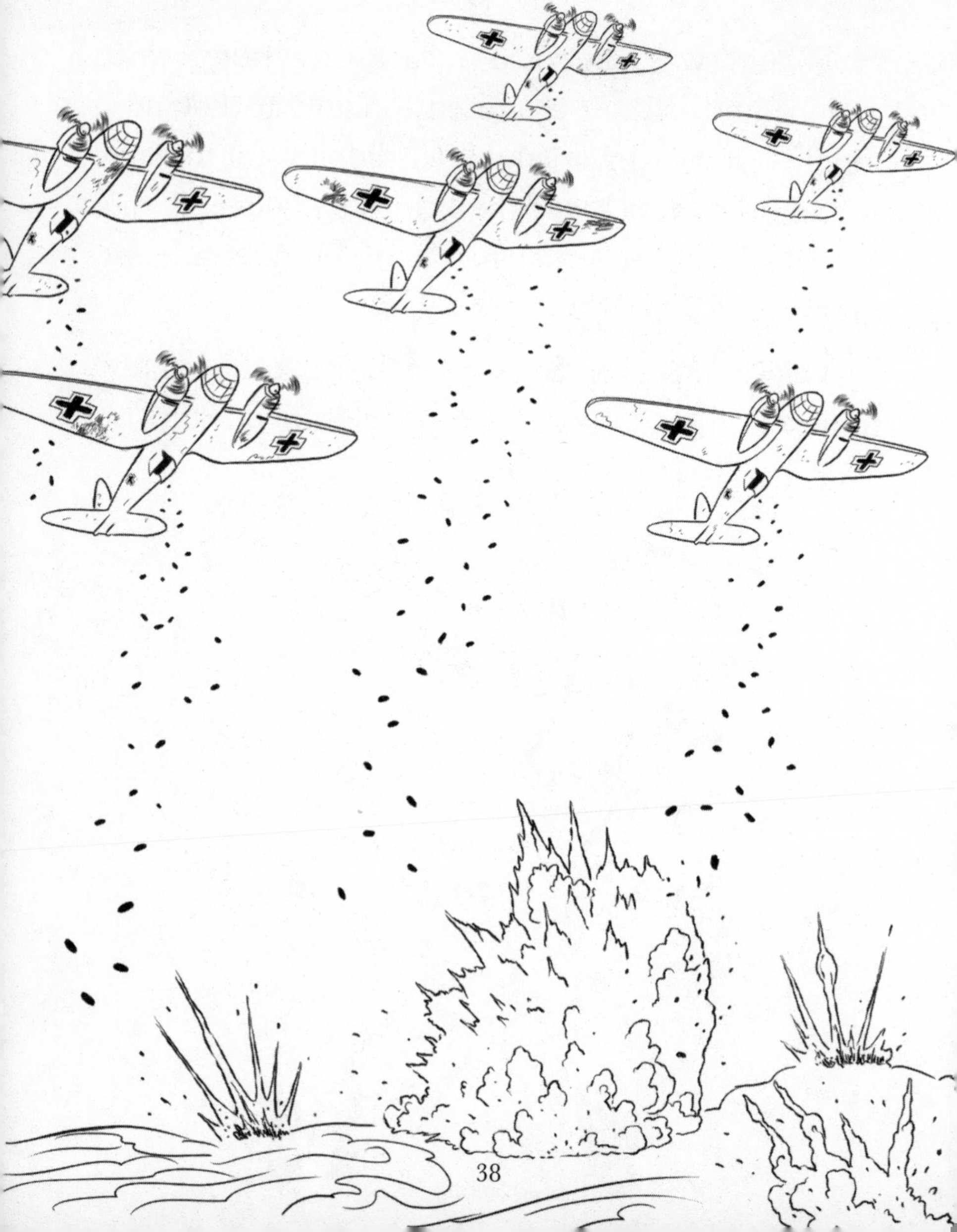

The Blitzkrieg Style of Warfare

The term "blitzkrieg" describes a military tactic used by the Nazis in the war. Blitzkrieg is a German word meaning "lightning war," and is characterized by speed, the element of surprise, and tremendous firepower from land and air. The idea was to catch the enemy unprepared and overwhelm them.

The Nazis weren't the only ones to employ a blitzkrieg strategy. The Allies also used it successfully against German troops later in the war.

The War in Europe

World War II had three main theaters, or areas involved directly in the war: Europe, Africa, and the Pacific.

Here are some of the key events in Europe during the first years of the war:

- After Germany invaded Poland on September 1, 1939, France and Britain declared war on Germany.

- Soon after, Canada, Australia, New Zealand, South Africa, and India entered the war on the side of France and Britain (the Allied powers).

- On September 16, the Soviet Union also invaded Poland. On September 28, Germany and the Soviet Union agreed to split Poland between them.

- The Soviet Union took over Latvia, Lithuania, Estonia, and Finland over the course of 1939 and 1940.

- Between April and June of 1940, Germany occupied Norway, Denmark, Belgium, the Netherlands, and Luxembourg.

- In May of 1940, German troops entered France. They reached Paris in mid June. On June 22, France agreed to let the Germans take over part (but not all) of their country.

- Italy joined the war as an Axis Power on June 10, 1940.

- July of 1940 marked the start of the Battle of Britain.
  Germany began bombing British ports, towns,
  and cities from warplanes. They targeted civilians
  in London and elsewhere to try to get the British
  government to give up. The British sent up their own
  fighter pilots to shoot down the German planes. The
  Germans continued bombing Britain until May of
  1941. (The Germans and British also fought at sea.)

- Despite the fact that they had a treaty, Germany began invading and attacking the Soviet Union starting in June of 1941. An estimated two million lives were lost during this nearly two-year siege. The Soviets finally forced the Germans to surrender after a five-month battle in the city of Stalingrad (now Volgograd). The Germans' defeat at the Battle of Stalingrad was devastating to them and marked a turning point in the overall war.

When the United States officially entered the war on December of 1941, it would have a profound impact on the war in Europe—and in the rest of the world.

Anti-Semitism
and the Holocaust

Anti-Semitism is a hatred of or prejudice against Jews. When Hitler took over Germany in 1933, he created policies and laws that discriminated against Jews. He ordered a boycott of Jewish-owned businesses. (A "boycott" is a ban on using something.) Jews were fired from government jobs and kept out of schools. Anti-Semitic mobs burned books that were considered to be "un-Germanic." Jews were stripped of German citizenship and were not allowed to marry German citizens.

On November 9 and 10 of 1938, mobs burned Jewish synagogues and broke the windows of Jewish-owned stores all over Germany. The Nazis then arrested thousands of Jews and sent them to concentration camps. This terrible event came to be known as Kristallnacht, or "Night of Broken Glass."

The Nazi concentration camps were massive prisonlike centers where Jews and other "enemies of Germany" were kept against their will. Prisoners were forced to perform hard labor. Many died from overwork, starvation, or disease. Later, they were murdered outright.

The Holocaust of WWII was the killing of an estimated six million Jews and millions of others by the Nazi government during the course of the war. (While many of the Nazis' victims were Jewish, they targeted other groups as well, including priests, gay people, and those with mental or physical disabilities.)

The Holocaust came to an end when the Allies won the war in 1945. The Allied troops freed the surviving prisoners in the camps.

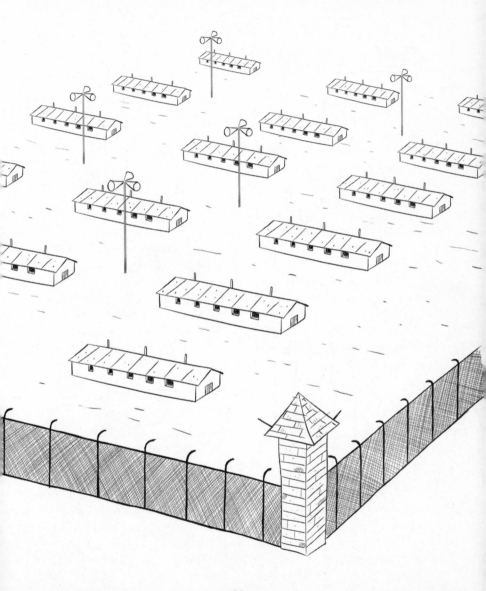

Anne Frank

Anne Frank was a young Jewish girl who lived in Germany during the war. After Hitler came into power, she and her family moved to Amsterdam, a city in the Netherlands, for safety.

But Hitler's troops took over the Netherlands in 1940, and starting in 1942, they began sending the Jews there to concentration camps. So Anne, her family, and four other people went into hiding in an annex, or extra rooms, above her father's office. For two years, they shared the small space and hid from the Nazis.

Anne kept a diary the whole time. After the war, her diary was published as *The Diary of a Young Girl.* Her story enabled readers to learn what it was like to be a young person during the Holocaust.

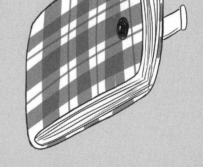

In 1944, the gestapo (the Nazi police) discovered the Franks' secret annex and arrested everyone. Anne and her sister were sent to a concentration camp, where they died of typhus, a disease. The only one to survive the camps was Anne's father.

The building containing the secret annex was turned into a museum called the Anne Frank House.

Oskar Schindler and Other Heroes

Many heroic individuals helped and protected Jews during the war. Here are just a few of them:

Oskar Schindler was a German businessman who saved more than a thousand Jews by employing them in his factory. He was a member of the Nazi party and used his position as well as bribes to make sure his Jewish employees weren't sent away to the camps.

Irena Sendler was a Polish social worker who rescued around twenty-five hundred Jewish children in Warsaw using fake birth certificates and other means.

Chiune Sugihara was a Japanese diplomat stationed in Lithuania who saved more than six thousand Jews. When the Nazis threatened to invade Lithuania, Sugihara and his wife stayed up for several days and nights frantically issuing visas for Jews to travel to Japan.

Raoul Wallenberg was a Swedish businessman and diplomat who saved around a hundred thousand Hungarian Jews. Using false passports and other documents, he kept them from being sent to concentration camps.

The War in Africa

Between 1940 and 1943, a number of battles took place in North Africa. Here are some of the key conflicts and campaigns:

- Italy entered World War II on June 10, 1940. A few days later, Allied troops entered the northern African country of Libya to seize an Italian military fort. This began a series of campaigns by the Allies and Axis to gain, or keep, control of various territories, including the Suez Canal (which connects the Mediterranean Sea and the Red Sea).

- The Italians invaded Egypt in September of 1940. The Allies managed to drive them back into Libya.

GERMANY

ITALY

TUNISIA

SUEZ CANAL

LIBYA

EGYPT

- In February of 1941, Hitler sent troops to North Africa to help the Italians, and they managed to push the Allies back into Egypt.

- In November of 1942, Allied troops forced the enemy west into Tunisia.

- In May of 1943, the Allies closed in on the Axis troops from the east and the west and defeated them. A quarter of a million Axis troops surrendered.

Resistance Fighters

Resistance fighters are people who organize with one another to resist, or fight against, an occupying force or government.

There were many resistance movements during World War II. Two famous examples are the Free French and the Free Danes. Free French troops fought with the British in Libya, Egypt, Syria, and Lebanon; they went on to fight in Italy, France, and elsewhere. In Denmark, the Free Danes resisted the German occupation of their country; they also saved the lives of thousands of Danish Jews by helping them to escape to Sweden.

The War in the Pacific

Japan and China had been at war since 1937, but Japan's interests in expanding its empire went beyond China and into the entire Pacific region.

Here are some of the key events of the war in the Pacific:

- Japan had set its sights on islands in the Pacific and in Southeast Asia that were controlled by France, Great Britain, and the Netherlands. In 1940 and 1941, Japan invaded French Indochina (which is now Vietnam, Laos, and Cambodia).

- In 1941 and 1942, Japan attacked the Philippines, which was a U.S. territory. In May of 1942, the Philippines surrendered.

- On December 7, 1941, Japanese warplanes attacked the American naval base in Pearl Harbor, Hawaii. The Japanese killed more than two thousand U.S. troops and damaged or destroyed many aircraft and battleships. On December 8, the United States declared war on Japan. A few days later, both Germany and Italy declared war on the U.S.

- Between 1942 and 1945, Japanese troops conquered and occupied Singapore, Burma (now Myanmar), and the Netherlands Indies (now Indonesia).

- In May and June of 1945, Allied powers defeated the Japanese in the Battle of Coral Sea and the Battle of Midway. Even so, the Japanese still controlled a large part of the Pacific.

BLAST BACK!

Espionage, Spies, and Code Breakers

Espionage is the using of spies to get information, or intelligence, for military or other purposes. During the war, many governments set up organizations to do espionage work.

Communicating by cipher, or code, was one way for the Allied powers and Axis powers to

keep their military plans a secret from each other. Skilled code-breakers were employed to decipher the enemies' codes and figure out what they were up to. The United States deciphered the Japanese code before the attack on Pearl Harbor (although they weren't able to prevent it).

One famous code-breaker was a British math-
ematician named Alan Turing. Turing helped
the British government decipher the German
codes. His work enabled the Allies to anticipate
the Germans' next military moves.

America and the War

The United States did not officially enter the war until the Japanese attacked Pearl Harbor in December of 1941. Before that, the nation was torn between an "interventionist" policy (which meant that it had a duty to help other countries with their problems and conflicts) and an "isolationist" policy (which meant that it should just keep to itself).

Franklin Delano Roosevelt, the U.S. president, was in favor of an interventionist policy. But many Americans felt that the terrible things happening in the rest of the world were faraway matters that did not affect them directly. Still, the United States did help in the war effort early on in many ways such as providing supplies to the Allies.

The United States also prepared for war in case it might eventually reach its shores. In September of 1939, President Roosevelt issued a "limited national emergency" in order to increase the size of the U.S. military. A year later, a draft was put in place to further increase the numbers. This draft required all men between the ages of twenty-one and thirty-six to sign up to fight if and when it became necessary.

The war finally reached American shores with Pearl Harbor. The U.S. government had to mobilize quickly. The country was suddenly part of a massive war that had multiple fronts all around the globe. Not only did the government have to recruit, draft, and train millions of soldiers; it had to boost production of military supplies and equipment.

The U.S. government had also started a secret project called the Manhattan Project. In 1939, a physicist named Albert Einstein had written a letter to President Roosevelt warning him that the Germans were developing a weapon called the atomic bomb. Soon after, President Roosevelt put in motion the events that would lead to an American atomic bomb. Scientists worked in complete secrecy to develop the technology for the bomb. Several facilities around the country were assigned to create enough plutonium and uranium (which are dangerous and unstable chemical elements) to power the bomb.

By July of 1945, the Manhattan Project had
produced an atomic bomb. It was tested at an
unpopulated site in New Mexico. When the
bomb exploded, the force was tremendous—
around two thousand times more powerful
than any other bomb at the time.

The Home Front

With so many goods to produce, and so many men away at war, millions of jobs opened up in factories and elsewhere. The unemployment problems of the Great Depression practically disappeared. Professional opportunities opened up for women, African Americans, and other minorities.

But the war required sacrifices, too. Women had to run their homes and take care of their families without their husbands and other male family members. There were shortages of food, housing, and other essentials.

There were shortages of nonessentials, too. For example, sugar had to be saved for American soldiers who wanted gum, chocolate bars, and other sweets; also, sugarcane was needed to produce gunpowder and dynamite.

Japanese American Internment Camps

In February of 1942, President Roosevelt signed an order that required Japanese Americans living in the United States to leave their homes and become prisoners in an internment, or detention, camp. Between 1942 and 1945, more than a hundred thousand Japanese Americans were forced to stay in ten different camps in the states of California, Wyoming, Arkansas, Utah, Colorado, and Arizona. The order was based on the government's racism and fear that these Japanese Americans might do something to hurt the U.S. war effort.

In 1988, Congress issued a formal apology to the victims of these camps.

The Final Years of the War

In July of 1943, the Italian dictator Mussolini was removed from power by Italy's king, Victor Emmanuel III, and the fascist government fell. In September of 1943, Italy surrendered to the Allies.

On June 6, 1944, nearly 160,000 Allied troops from the United States, Britain, and Canada began a campaign to drive the Germans out of Western Europe. (This day is called D-day.) The Allies landed on the beaches of Normandy, France, and fought their way inland against the Germans. By August, Allied troops had freed the city of Paris and the rest of northern France.

The Allies continued their way toward Germany. In Ardennes (a forested area in Western Europe) the Germans made a surprise attack on the Allies. This battle—the Battle of the Bulge—lasted from December 1944 to January 1945, with the Allies eventually defeating the Germans.

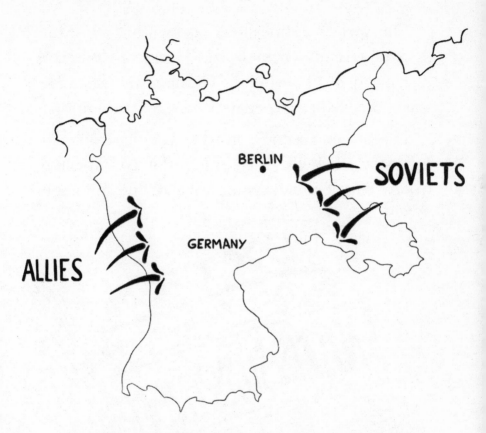

By February, things looked very bad for the Germans. In March, the Allies moved into Germany from the west. Soviet troops moved in from the east. There was no way for the Germans to win the war.

On April 25, Hitler took his own life. On May 8, the Germans surrendered. (President Roosevelt died on April 12, before the German surrender. He was succeeded by President Harry S. Truman.)

In the meantime, on the Pacific front, in February of 1943, U.S. troops forced Japanese troops out of Guadalcanal (one of the Solomon

Islands). In July of 1944, Americans captured Saipan (one of the Mariana Islands) and used it as a base for their fighter planes to bomb Japan. In March of 1945, the Americans under General Douglas MacArthur occupied Manila (the capital city of the Philippines). Around the same time, the Americans took control of two Japanese-owned islands, Iwo Jima and Okinawa.

The United States wanted to end the war with Japan once and for all. On August 6, 1945, under orders from President Truman, an American plane dropped an atomic bomb on the Japanese city of Hiroshima. Three days later, the Americans dropped another atomic bomb on the city of Nagasaki. No one knows exactly how many people died in the two bombings, but the number is well over one hundred thousand. On September 2, Japan surrendered.

The Legacy of the War

World War II was the biggest war the world had ever known. More people died in that war than in any other war. After the end of the war, all the countries involved had the enormous task of repairing the damage, healing, and moving forward.

Months before the war was actually over, Allied leaders met at two conferences, the Yalta Conference and the Potsdam Conference, to figure out what to do after the war ended. The matters to be decided included: the reestablishment of boundaries, rebuilding devastated cities and economies, and reparations (or making amends) to victims of the war.

A number of things happened after the war as a result of these conferences. The Allies took over Germany and began a program of complete reconstruction. German-occupied lands were taken away from them, and the German citizens within them forcibly removed. Many German factories were destroyed. The process of denazification was implemented to remove all Nazi influence.

The Allies also took over Japan. Led by General Douglas MacArthur, the occupying forces were charged with punishing, reforming, and rebuilding Japan. Among other things, the Japanese were stripped of their army. (The occupation lasted until 1952.)

In 1945 and 1946, a special tribunal, or court, was created to try Nazi leaders as war criminals. (War criminals are soldiers and military leaders who break the rules of warfare.) The tribunal was made up of representatives from the United States, Great Britain, the Soviet Union, and France. The trials are known as the Nuremberg Trials.

Three of the twenty-two on trial—the defendants—
were found not guilty. The other nineteen
defendants were found guilty for starting the war
and for other crimes. (There were other similar
trials after World War II, including the trial of
twenty eight political and military leaders in
Tokyo, Japan, from 1946 to 1948.)

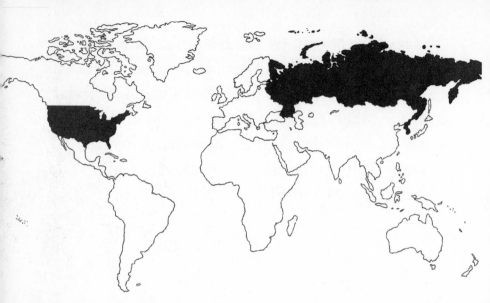

World War II had also created two new super-powers: the United States and the Soviet Union. Unfortunately, these countries also became enemies. The Soviet Union continued controlling the Eastern European countries that had been freed after the war and turned them into communist states. The United States did not want communism to spread. This rivalry between them was called the Cold War (although it wasn't an actual war) and dominated much of the rest of the century.

Today, many museums and memorial sites exist to remember World War II and honor its victims, including the United States Holocaust Memorial Museum in Washington, D.C., and the Hiroshima Peace Memorial Museum in Japan.

Well, it's been a great adventure. Good-bye, World War II!

Where to next?

Also available:

Selected Bibliography

The Boston Globe Online, https://www.bostonglobe.com/
metro/2013/11/04/boat-wreck-off-coast-dark-reminder-wwii
/OLUV9YOFdMDjfeu5VFIGHJ/story.html

BBC Online, news.bbc.co.uk/onthisday/hi/dates/stories/
december/11/newsid_3532000/3532401.stm

Encyclopedia Britannica Online, www.britannica.com

Encyclopedia Britannica Kids Online, www.kids.britannica.com

The National WWII Museum (New Orleans) Online,
www.nationalww2museum.org/learn/education/
for-students/ww2-history/america-goes-to-war.html

Operation Neptune: The Prelude to D-Day by David Wragg,
the History Press, 2014

Veteran Affairs Canada Online, http://www.veterans.gc.ca/
eng/remembrance/history/second-world-war/
battle-gulf-st-lawrence/intro

NANCY OHLIN is the author of the YA novels *Always*, *Forever* and *Beauty* as well as the early chapter book series Greetings from Somewhere under the pseudonym Harper Paris. She lives in Ithaca, New York, with her husband, their two kids, four cats, and assorted animals who happen to show up at their door. Visit her online at nancyohlin.com.

ROGER SIMÓ is an illustrator based in a town near Barcelona, where he lives with his wife, son, and daughter. He has become the person that he would have envied when he was a child: someone who makes a living by drawing and explaining fantastic stories.

ADAM LARKUM, the cover artist, is a freelance illustrator based in the United Kingdom. In his fifteen years of illustrating, he's worked on more than forty books. In addition to his illustration work, he also dabbles in animation and develops characters for television.